GALORE PARK

# So you really want to learn

# Junior History

# Book 1

### Edward Lawlor Brennan

Series Editor: Niall Murphy

www.galorepark.co.uk

Published by Galore Park Publishing Ltd
19/21 Sayers Lane, Tenterden, Kent TN30 6BW
www.galorepark.co.uk

Design and typography The Design Gallery, Suffolk
Illustrations by Gwyneth Williams, Rosie Brooks & Jane Humphries

Printed by Replika Press Pvt. Ltd., India

ISBN-13: 978 1 902984 96 4
ISBN-10: 1 902984 96 X

First published 2006, reprinted 2010

Accompanying this course:
A set of suggested answers to the exercises in this book is available from the publishers at www.galorepark.co.uk.

Details of other Galore Park publications are available at www.galorepark.co.uk
ISEB Revision Guides, publications and examination papers may also be obtained from Galore Park.

The publishers are grateful for permission to use the photographs and additional artwork as follows:
(T=Top, CT=Centre Top, B=Bottom, CB=Centre Bottom, L=Left, R=Right, C=Centre, CR =Centre Right, CL= Centre Left.) P5 T Geoff Brightling © Dorling Kindersley, CT Nigel Hicks © Dorling Kindersley, CB © Mike Kipling Photography / Alamy, B © Fridmar Damm/zefa/Corbis; P7 T image source, CT Janine Wiedel Photolibrary / Alamy, CB © Leeds Castle Foundation, B Peter Menzel / Science Photo Library; P8 Steve Gorton © Dorling Kindersley; P11 © The Trustees of the British Museum; P15 DAVID R. FRAZIER / SCIENCE PHOTO LIBRARY; P16 SCIENCE PHOTO LIBRARY; P19 © Dorling Kindersley; P22 TOM MCHUGH / SCIENCE PHOTO LIBRARY; P24 ADAM HART-DAVIS / SCIENCE PHOTO LIBRARY; P25 DE AGOSTINI EDITORE PICTURE LIBRARY, Peter Visscher © Dorling Kindersley; P29 © The Trustees of the British Museum The Flood Tablet, relating part of the Epic of Gilgamesh; P30 courtesy of Great Orme Mines Ltd; P31 T Courtesy of Great Orme Mines Ltd; P32 C © Catherine Karnow/CORBIS; P32 B © Andrew Pointer; P37 L © Sandro Vannini/CORBIS, R © Roger Wood/CORBIS; P38 © Dorling Kindersley, © Dorling Kindersley; P39 Oscar Dahl; P40 TOM MCHUGH / SCIENCE PHOTO LIBRARY; P42 © Royalty-Free/Corbis; P43 T © Visual Arts Library (London) / Alamy; P43 B © The Art Archive/ Corbis; P45 BRIAN BRAKE / SCIENCE PHOTO LIBRARY; P49 Copyright Chris Sloan, Courtesy J.M. Kenoyer, Copyright J.M. Kenoyer, Courtesy Dept. of Archeology and Museums, Govt. of Pakistan; P50 Andy Crawford © Dorling Kindersley, Courtesy of the National Museum, New Delhi; P52 B Frank Greenaway © Dorling Kindersley; P52 T © CHINA NEWSPHOTO/ Reuters/Corbis; P55 William Donahue © Dorling Kindersley; P56 © The Trustees of the British Museum; P57 T Courtesy of Maksim; P61 Time Life Pictures/Getty Images, Peter Dennis © Dorling Kindersley; P65 © Archivo Iconografico, S.A./CORBIS; P66 DE AGOSTINI EDITORE PICTURE LIBRARY, Maltings Partnership © Dorling Kindersley; P70 © The Trustees of the British Museum

# Contents

# Chapter 5 Ancient Egypt

# Chapter 6 The spread of civilisation

## Chapter 7 The Iron Age

## Chapter 8 The Greek Dark Ages

# Introduction

Along with reading, writing and arithmetic, history is often referred to as the fourth R – the right to remember. Children and adults have a deep desire to know where they come from; history is the subject that deals with that need.

Telling stories is one of the most important methods in teaching history. Good stories have a beginning, middle and end. The story of Britain from Stone Age times is an interesting and exciting story. In Book 1 of the course we aim to tell that story in a coherent, chronological way. This provides a useful preparation for the skills required as a young historian such as the interpretation of evidence, while instilling a love and fascination for the study of the past.

Edward Lawlor Brennan

2006

# Chapter 1
# History – The story of the past

## When did that happen?

When we study history we learn about things that happened in the past. The past may be a short time ago or a long time ago. It could be a day, a week or a year ago. It could be a number of years ago or even longer than that.

- Has anything interesting or unusual happened to you in the last week?

- How long ago did it happen?

- What has been the most important event in your life so far?

- How long ago did that happen?

The answers you give to these questions are part of your life story, part of history.

Read the following passage about a boy called Nigel. In it he tells us about his life. Although it is not very long, he is telling us his life history.

My name is Nigel and I am nine years old. My sister's name is Emma. She is two years old. I learned to walk when I was one year old. At the age of two I broke my mother's favourite cup and she was not very pleased. When I was four I went to playschool. I loved to colour pictures and play with toys when I was there. A year later I went to primary school. When I was six years old we went to live in London. My sister Emma was born when I was seven. At the age of eight I learned to play the piano. Last year my football team won the cup and I won a medal.

Nigel's story is shown on the black time line below. It tells what age Nigel was when the events happened. Below the line is a red time line, which shows how long ago the events took place.

## Nigel's Age

| 0 | 1 | 2 | 3 | 4 | 5 | 6 | 7 | 8 | 9 |
|---|---|---|---|---|---|---|---|---|---|

*Nigel born*  *Learned to walk*  *Broke cup*  *Went to playschool*  *Primary school*  *Moved to London*  *Emma born*  *Learned piano / won medal*  *Now*

| 9 | 8 | 7 | 6 | 5 | 4 | 3 | 2 | 1 | 0 |
|---|---|---|---|---|---|---|---|---|---|

Number of years ago

The next time line gives us more information about Nigel's family. It goes back further in time.

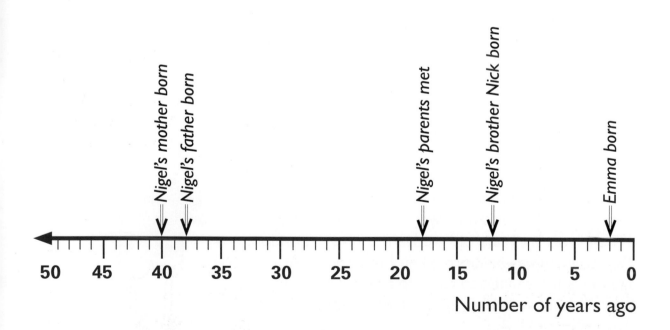

Number of years ago

# A.D. and B.C.

History is about the past. In this book we shall be learning about things that happened a long, long time ago. We shall be learning about things that happened thousands of years ago, before the birth of Jesus Christ. Jesus Christ was born in Palestine just over two thousand years ago.

The pyramids B.C.

- Things that happened before the birth of Christ are said to have happened in the years **B.C.** (before Christ).

A Greek temple B.C.

- Things that happened after the birth of Christ are said to have happened in the years **A.D.**, or Anno Domini. (Anno Domini is Latin and means 'in the Year of our Lord'.)

So, all times in history are counted as being either before or after the birth of Christ.

A Norman church A.D.

- 2000 B.C. means two thousand years before Christ was born.

- 2000 A.D. means two thousand years after Christ was born.

Windsor Castle A.D.

Imagine a child born in the year 2005. The child was born 2005 years after Jesus was born. Now imagine a child born in the year 1500 B.C. How long ago was that? If he were still alive today, how much older would the child born in 1500 B.C. be than the one born in 2005 A.D.?

You can work it out like this:

How many years between 1500 B.C. and 2005 A.D.?

Number of years before the birth of Christ (B.C.) = 1500

Number of years after the birth of Christ (A.D.) = 2005

Total number of years                                     3505

So a child born in 1500 B.C. would be 3505 years older than a child born in 2005 A.D.!

# Time lines

When we are learning about things that happened a long time ago, time lines can be very useful. The time line below helps us to understand how long ago things happened. The red section shows us the years before the birth of Christ. The blue section shows us the years after the birth of Christ.

## B.C.                                                                           A.D.

| 1500 | 753 | 0 | 1066 | 1509 | 2000 |
|------|-----|---|------|------|------|
|      | Foundation of Rome | Birth of Christ | Battle of Hastings | Henry VIII becomes King |      |

Copy the time line and add the following dates to it. Make sure you put them on the right side of the line:

**2000 B.C.**          **1700 B.C.**          **500 B.C.**          **55 B.C.**

**55 A.D.**          **1200 A.D.**          **1750 A.D.**          **1999 A.D.**

Remember, the B.C. dates will be on the left of the page, and the A.D. dates will be on the right.

# Learning about the past

A historian is someone who studies the past (history). How do historians learn about what happened in the past? They can ask someone, but that is no good if the thing happened a long time ago and there is no one alive to ask. They can read about it in a book, but how did the writer of the book find out what happened? Who did he or she ask?

There are lots of ways in which we can find out about the past:

- We learn about events in the past from the **stories** we hear from our parents and grandparents.

- We learn about the past from **books**, **newspapers**, **pictures** and **photos**. We might find these in a **library**.

- We learn about the past from **buildings** like churches, castles and towers which tell us much about the way people lived.

- We learn about the past from **everyday objects** which have survived from that time. We might see these objects in a **museum**.

# Archaeology

**Archaeologists** investigate the lives of people from the past by studying the objects these people left behind. These objects could include buildings, artwork, tools, bones and pottery. Archaeologists might make an exciting discovery, like finding the tomb of Tutankhamun (see page 41), or they might learn about people in the past by studying a few stone tools or seeds that have survived from ancient times.

A place where archaeological evidence is found is called a **site**. When archaeologists excavate or dig up a site, they sometimes find **artefacts**.

Artefacts are objects that have been made by people.

Archaeologists, like historians, want to know about the past. For example, they might try to find out why ancient people stopped hunting and switched to farming, or why people started to live in cities instead of in small groups.

Archeologists excavating a site

# Evidence: Primary and secondary

As we have seen, historians find out about the past by looking at things such as books, photographs, buildings and artefacts. All of this is **evidence**. Just as Sherlock Holmes looked at evidence to find out who committed a crime, historians look at evidence to find out about the past.

Most historians follow the same steps in their work. First they select for study a topic, period or person from the past. Then they read as much as possible about the subject and finally they write an account of it.

Historians use two main types of evidence in their research: **primary sources** and **secondary sources**.

- Primary sources are documents produced during the period being studied. They include books, diaries, letters and government records written by people who were there at the time.

- Secondary sources are materials prepared later by people who studied primary sources.

Historians prefer to use primary sources because they are likely to get a better account of what happened from people who were there at the time. Why do you think this is?

# Who to believe? Bias in history

Evidence has to be looked at carefully because different people interpret the past in different ways. It is important to be fair to all sides when telling the story of the past. Historians often agree about certain facts but they don't always agree about the meaning or importance of these facts.

Sometimes people have a view which is **biased**. For example a football supporter will normally say that his or her favourite team played really well, even if it didn't. This is because he or she is biased. An English newspaper report of the Gulf War in the Middle East might suggest that the British and American troops invaded Iraq to restore peace in the country; an Iraqi newspaper report might suggest that the British and American troops were invaders and should be expelled. The difference between the two views may be one caused by bias.

So who should we believe? When studying history, we need to be aware that the views expressed by people, whether at the time or later, may be biased.

# Using evidence: Case study

Compare these two letters about life in the trenches during the First World War. Which do you think gives the 'truth'? Why do you think Arthur's letter to his mother is so different from Albert Powis's letter to his friend?

1. Arthur to his mother

Dear Mother,

We arrived in France a few days ago. There were flags and flowers everywhere. People were giving us cigarettes and chocolates. Everyone was singing and the atmosphere was electric. We took the train to the front line and then we marched to our trenches. The trenches are comfortable and safe and we have lots of food. I had plenty of turnip and potato soup and lots of meat today. I'm in very good health and I hope the same can be said of everyone at home.

Yours faithfully,

Arthur

2. Albert Powis to a friend

> *Our trenches were filthy dirty. Every time it rained our latrine would overflow and the rats that went in there were as big as tom cats. The place was very uncomfortable and the soldiers were plagued by lice. Lice, dirt, heat, cold, mud, rats, foul smells; this was life in the trenches.*
>
> Albert Powis

# Exercise 1.1

Read Nigel's story on pages 3 and 4. Look at the first time line on page 4, and answer the following questions. How long ago is it since:

1. Nigel started to learn the piano?

2. Nigel's team won the cup?

3. Emma was born?

4. Nigel went to playschool?

5. Nigel learned to walk?

6. Nigel was born?

7. Nigel broke his mother's favourite cup?

8. Nigel went to primary school?

9. The family moved to London?

10. Nigel won a medal?

Now draw a time line of the important events that have happened in your family since you were born.

# Exercise 1.2

Look at the second time line on page 4 and answer the questions below:

1. How long ago did Nigel's parents meet?

2. What age is Nigel's father?

3. How many years is it since Nick was born?

4. How many years is it since Nigel's mother was born?

5. How many children are there in Nigel's family?

. . . . . . . . . . . . . . . . . . . . . . . . . . . . . . . . . . . . . . . . . . . . . . . . . . . .

# Exercise 1.3

Look at this artefact and answer the questions about it:

1. What do you think this artefact was used for?

2. What was it made from?

3. Is it natural or man–made?

4. How was it made?

5. Is there writing/decoration on it?

6. What do you think was the purpose of the decoration?

7. Does the artefact tell us anything about the owner?

8. What might have happened to this artefact after it was used?

9. Where might you see an item like this today?

10. Draw and decorate a similar artefact.

. . . . . . . . . . . . . . . . . . . . . . . . . . . . . . . . . . . . . . . . . . . . . . . . . . . .

# To do

• Choose a subject that you are interested in. It could be your favourite sport, a holiday resort, a pop group or even your school. Write a summary of the subject you have chosen, saying clearly why you like it. Add some pictures or photographs.

• Then find the views of someone who does not agree with you. Add their views to your project. Try to understand why their view is different from yours.

• Finally, look again at the views that you began with. Do you still think the same about your topic? Have you changed your mind?

# Chapter 2
# The time of the dinosaurs

## Terrible lizards

We are now going to begin our journey into the past. We are going to travel back in time, not just a few hundred years, or a few thousand years. We are going back hundreds of millions of years, to the time when the **dinosaurs** lived on earth. The word 'dinosaur' comes from two Greek words meaning 'terrible lizard'. Dinosaurs were reptiles that lived on earth over two hundred million years ago. A reptile is an animal with dry scaly skin which breathes through its lungs. It lays eggs on land. Dinosaurs roamed the earth for about one hundred and fifty million years. They lived in most parts of the world and in different surroundings, from swamps to dry land. Other dinosaur-like reptiles lived in the seas or flew through the air like birds.

## Where they came from

So, where did the dinosaurs come from? The first creatures with a backbone were **fish** that lived in the seas and swamps. As millions of years passed the bodies of fish changed. Some fish grew very strong fins and used their fins to crawl out of the water onto land. This happened about 400 million years ago. Later, some creatures began to live on land all the time because there was plenty of food. They were able to lay eggs on land. The eggshells were hard and waterproof. These creatures were the first reptiles and they looked like lizards. They were the ancestors of the dinosaurs and were **amphibians**. Amphibians are animals with moist, shiny skin which can live on land or in water. They lay their eggs in water or in swampy ground. A frog is an amphibian.

# The dinosaur world

When the dinosaurs lived, hundreds of millions of years ago, the earth was very different from the way it is today. Scientists believe that the seven continents (Asia, Africa, Antarctica, Australasia, Europe, North America and South America) were all joined up and surrounded by an enormous sea. Some areas were dry and rocky and had no plants. Other areas had large forests of cone-bearing trees. There were also mosses and ferns, some of which were as tall as trees. Plant-eating dinosaurs fed on these plants.

If you had been around at that time, here are some of the dinosaurs that you would have seen:

**Brachiosaurus** (Bracky-oh-sore-us) was a giant plant-eating dinosaur. It could eat food from high up on tall plants which could not be reached by other dinosaurs.

**Deinonychus** (Die-non-ee-kuss) was much smaller, but was a fierce hunter. Its large jaws and sharp teeth were ideal for tearing meat. It could run very fast on its long slender legs, and its big tail kept it balanced. This dinosaur probably hunted in packs.

**Tyrannosaurus rex** (Ti-ran-oh-sore-us rex) was one of the largest of the dinosaurs (rex means 'king' in Latin). It was a meat-eater which used its powerful claws and sharp teeth when hunting its prey. It could open its mouth very wide and swallow large lumps of meat.

**Stegosaurus** (Steg-oh-sore-us) was a plant-eating animal. Its front legs were shorter than its back legs. This made it easier for it to feed on plants close to the ground. The bony plates along its back helped to protect it from attack. The spikes at the end of its tail were probably used to drive away its enemies.

**Apatosaurus** (A-pat-oh-sore-us) had a large body and a small head. It was a plant-eater and probably lived in herds. It moved slowly on its short, thick legs. Its powerful tail was used to defend itself.

**Triceratops** (Try-ser-a-tops) was also a plant-eater and had an enormous head. The bony collar protected its neck from its enemies, such as Tyrannosaurus rex.

**Pteranodon** (Te-ran-oh-don) was a flying reptile. It fed on fish which it caught in its large beak.

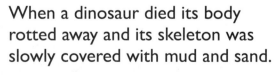

If you have seen the film *Jurassic Park*, you will have seen some of these dinosaurs. You may have thought that they were imaginary monsters, but dinosaurs were real creatures who really lived on earth, many millions of years ago. If you visit the Natural History Museum in London, the first thing you will see as you enter the building is the skeleton of a huge dinosaur.

## How we know about dinosaurs

Two hundred years ago, no one had even heard of dinosaurs. At that time some dinosaur bones were found buried in rocks. Imagine how surprised people must have been to find the bones of such huge animals! The remains of animals or plants, found buried in the rock, are called **fossils**. So how did the dinosaur turn into a fossil?

When a dinosaur died its body rotted away and its skeleton was slowly covered with mud and sand.

Over millions of years, the mud and sand hardened and changed into rock. Later still these layers of rock were covered with soil and other materials.

Then, as the wind and rain gradually wore away the ground level, things that had been buried deep under the ground came to the surface. In this way, scientists were able to find layers of rock which contained the fossils of dinosaurs.

When the bones of dinosaurs are found, they must be taken out of the ground very carefully. Drills, small chisels and brushes are used to remove the rock from around the fossil.

Tyrannosaurus rex skeleton supported by a frame

Fossil bones break easily, so they are wrapped in cloth and plaster for protection. Then they are put into boxes and taken to a museum. At the museum, the bones are cleaned and any broken pieces are repaired. Missing bones are replaced with new pieces made from fibreglass, plastic or plaster. The bones are coated with varnish to give them extra protection and strength.

When everything is ready, the skeleton is put together. A metal frame is used to hold the bones of the skeleton in position.

## The end of the dinosaurs

Nobody knows for certain why the dinosaurs died out but scientists have many theories. One theory is that about 65 million years ago the weather suddenly grew cooler. Temperatures dropped and much of the earth was frozen over. Dinosaurs were too big to **hibernate** in dens. They had no fur or feathers to keep themselves warm, and so they died. Another theory is that a huge **asteroid** hit the earth. This caused a huge cloud of smoke and dust to rise up and black out the sunlight for many months. Plants stopped growing and died away. The plant-eating dinosaurs starved and died. The meat-eating dinosaurs which fed on them also died.

# Charles Darwin

According to the Bible, the world was created in six days.

**Day 1**: God created Day and Night.

**Day 2**: God created Heaven and Earth.

**Day 3**: God created the Seas and the Dry Land.

**Day 4**: God created the Sun and the Moon.

**Day 5**: God created Fish to live in the Seas and Birds to live on the Dry Land.

**Day 6**: God created Animals and Man.

For hundreds of years, people believed that the world as we know it really was created over a six-day period, with God resting on the seventh day. What is more, by studying the Bible, which tells us the names and ages of the men who lived between Adam (the first Man) and Jesus Christ, scholars tried to estimate exactly when the world began. James Ussher, Bishop of Armagh, who wrote from 1648-1654, calculated that the precise moment of creation was at nightfall before Monday 23$^{rd}$ October 4004 B.C. and, from that time, Bibles were printed with dates in the margin.

Charles Darwin

Charles Darwin, a British naturalist who lived from 1809 to 1882, challenged these ideas. Darwin believed that all species had **evolved** from a few earlier ones. It was Darwin who first suggested that humans evolved from apes. His **theory of evolution** shocked many people of his day because they believed that God had created each **species** exactly as they are today. Darwin proved that the various species had evolved or changed over hundreds of thousands of years, and that they are still evolving.

Darwin's theories were supported by the development of a new science, **geology** (the study of rocks), which proved that the world was much older than Biblical scholars had claimed.

Today there are some people who still believe that God created the world in six days. They are called **Creationists** and they reject the views of Darwin and other scientists.

# Exercise 2.1

Read the information on pages 12 to 15 and answer the following questions:

1. What is a dinosaur?

2. Where does the name come from?

3. How long ago did dinosaurs live on earth?

4. When did the first creature crawl out of the sea?

5. What is an amphibian?

6. Describe the world as it was in dinosaur times.

7. Describe the following dinosaurs: (a) Brachiosaurus,
   (b) Tyrannosaurus rex, (c) Stegosaurus and (d) Pteranodon.

8. Where might you go to see the skeleton of a dinosaur?

. . . . . . . . . . . . . . . . . . . . . . . . . . . . . . . . . . . . . . . . . . . .

# Exercise 2.2

Read the information on pages 14 to 15 and fill in the sentences below:

1. It is almost _____ years since people first learned that dinosaurs had ever existed.

2. The remains of animals or plants, found buried in the rock, are called _____.

3. When a dinosaur died, its skeleton was slowly covered with _____ and _____.

4. When the _____ of dinosaurs are found, they must be taken out of the ground very carefully using drills and _____ to remove the rock from around the fossil.

5. In the museum, the dinosaur's bones are coated with _____ to give them extra protection and strength.

6. Some scientists believe that dinosaurs died out about _____ years ago when temperatures _____ and much of the earth was _____.

# Exercise 2.3

Read the information on page 16 about Charles Darwin and explain the following words in your own sentences (you may need to use a dictionary or the Internet to help you):

1. naturalist

2. evolution

3. species

4. geology

5. creationist

# To do

- Make a dinosaur from plasticine or modelling clay.

- Why do you think dinosaurs disappeared? Write a story about the day the dinosaurs died out.

- Make a poster to display in your classroom, showing all the dinosaurs you have learnt about.

- Design three new dinosaurs. Draw a picture of each and give it a name. Describe what sort of creature each one is.

# Chapter 3
# The Stone Age

## Prehistoric man

The earliest people who lived on earth are called **prehistoric** people. They lived long before writing was invented. We have learned about these people from their tools and weapons. We have also learned about them from their paintings and from fossils. (Fossils as you learned in Chapter 2 are the hardened remains of animals or plants.)

As we saw in Chapter 2, Darwin produced considerable evidence that men and apes come from the same ancestor and evolved into separate species around 20 million years ago. The first 'man' that we know about lived two million years ago: we call him **Southern Ape-man** and he lived in Africa. He had a small brain and features like an ape, but his body was upright like a man's. He was about four feet tall and walked on two legs, with his arms free. Pebble tools have been found at some sites where ape-men lived. They were probably used to skin and cut up antelope and other small animals.

About 500 000 years ago, Southern Ape-man began to die out, like the dinosaurs had before him, but a new type of man began to develop called **Erect man** or **homo erectus**. Erect man lived in southern Asia and parts of Europe as well as Africa. We know from remains found in caves near Beijing in China that he was about five feet tall. Although his face still looked like an ape's, his brain was twice the size of Southern Ape-man's. His hands were more flexible. Erect men used stone to make tools such as hand-axes and probably used wood to make clubs and spears. Because the climate was colder than in Africa, Erect man used fire for warmth and to frighten animals such as deer, antelope, elephant and rhinoceros into traps, allowing him to hunt them.

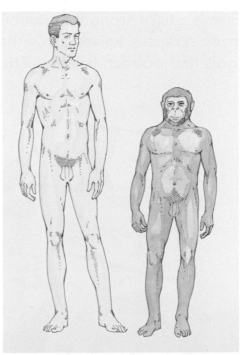

The difference between modern man and Erect man

# The Ice Ages

From before the time of Erect man until about 10 000 years ago, much of the earth was covered by ice. We call this the **Ice Age**. Ice sheets and glaciers, thousands of feet thick, covered Northern America, Europe and Asia. As each wave of ice spread across the earth, the human population shrank. During this period, wolves, mammoths and woolly rhinoceroses lived in Britain. Thousands of years later, the ice melted very gradually.

Although we usually refer to this period as the Ice Age, there were in fact four Ice Ages altogether. In between each one, the temperature became warmer. Archaeologists have found proof of an elephant living in Norfolk during one of these warmer periods.

# The Old Stone Age

After the Ice Age, man had to hunt wild animals and eat roots, nuts, fruits and berries to survive. Many of the tools and weapons he used were made of **stone**. Because of this, we call this period the **Old Stone Age**.

Old Stone Age people used **flint** to make many of their tools and weapons. Flint is a hard stone that can be sharpened easily. Old Stone Age people made scrapers, knives, arrow heads and axes from it. Some of their stone tools had wooden handles. They also made needles from **bone**.

Old Stone Age people had to follow their food supply, just as the Lapps of Scandinavia follow the reindeer today. They hunted small animals, birds, bison (a type of buffalo) and deer. They hunted for meat (to eat) and for skins (to make clothes). Sometimes, if they found a lake full of fish, they settled down and formed larger groups. They caught fish with **harpoons**. They made **rafts** to float on and, later, **canoes** from hollowed-out tree trunks. They trapped larger animals like the mammoth in deep pits and speared them to death. The wild dogs that followed the hunters for scraps of food were gradually tamed and trained to help in the hunt. As well as hunting, people gathered fruit, berries, leaves and plants. Because of the way they lived, these men are called **hunter gatherers**.

# Clothes and houses

Old Stone Age people did not build houses because they had to keep moving in search of food. They lived in **caves** or sheltered under trees and bushes. Later they built **huts** using animal skins and bones, as well as branches and leaves. They also made **clothes** from animal skins.

First they scraped the skin clean and dried it in the sun. Then they cut it into the required shape and sewed it together using a pointed needle made from bone. They used strips of animal skin as thread.

# Discoveries

Although many important changes took place in prehistoric times, the speed at which they happened was very slow. One of the most important discoveries made was how to use **fire**. We don't know for certain how this discovery was made. Perhaps it was discovered after lightning had started a forest fire, or someone might have noticed sparks when making flint tools. Fire was used by Old Stone Age people to heat their caves, frighten wild animals and cook their food.

Although these people did not write, they made beautiful **statues** of animals and people from bone or deer antlers. They also drew **paintings** in caves. More than a hundred decorated caves have been found in Europe. One of the best known is the cave of **Altamira** in northern Spain. Here, paintings of animals, people and hunting scenes were

Cave painting from Altamira in northern Spain

found, deep inside the caves. The Old Stone Age people had used black, yellow, red and white colours, which were obtained from charcoal, clay and crushed rocks.

# The New Stone Age

The **New Stone Age** (or **Neolithic** Age) started in about 8000 B.C. in the Near East. Around this time one of the greatest changes in the history of the human race took place.

It happened in the **Fertile Crescent**, which is an area on the banks of the Tigris and Euphrates rivers

(see map on page 27). It was a change in the way people obtained food. For the first time, people began growing their own crops so they did not have to wander in search of food supplies. They became **farmers** rather than hunters. The fertile soil provided them with crops of wheat, barley and oats. The wheat was cut with a flint **sickle**, a curved blade. Women pounded the grain into flour using a pair of **quern-stones** and baked flat loaves of bread on hot stones. Farmers tamed more and more animals such as sheep, cattle, goats and pigs. They seem to have chosen young and weak animals from wild herds. These would have been easier to catch and handle in captivity.

The end of the Ice Ages had meant that man was able to live throughout the world and three main types of man developed in the different parts of the world: dark-skinned people lived in central Africa; white-skinned people lived in north Africa, Europe and the Near East; and yellow-skinned people lived in Asia and America. At this time, America was joined to Asia, but as the ice melted at the end of the Ice Ages, rising sea levels cut Asia off from America.

A map to show how the three main types of man developed across the world

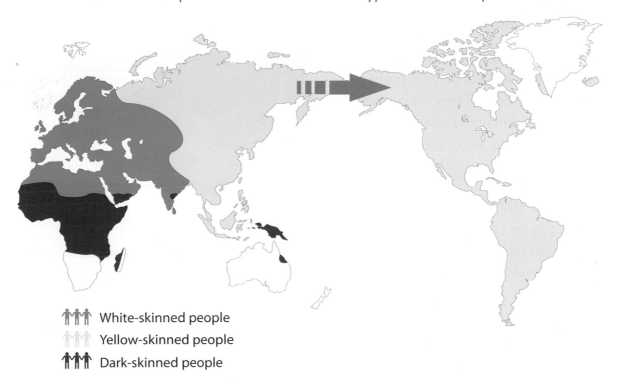

White-skinned people
Yellow-skinned people
Dark-skinned people

# The effects of farming

As a result of improvements in farming, the human population began to grow and many more people could live in a small area. Extra food could be traded for other goods. This was called **bartering**. Villages and towns grew up around trading centres. Because of less time spent hunting some people had more time to do other things. New discoveries were made, such as the making of **pottery**. Food could now be stored more easily. People began to work as smiths making things from metal and they became traders. **Spinning** and **weaving** were discovered and clothes began to be made from wool and linen. Houses were made from stones and wood and the roofs were thatched with reeds and straw.

# Stone Age Britain

Britain emerged from the last Ice Age around 8000 B.C. At that time, the British Isles were covered with ice and both Britain and Ireland were connected to the mainland of Europe. When the ice melted, the seas began to rise. Some of the land was covered with water and the countries as they are today were formed. Some people lived in caves in Britain and new settlers started to travel to Britain around this time. One group of settlers arrived from Denmark. Remains of their settlement have been found at Star Carr in North Yorkshire.

Shortly after 4000 B.C., tribes of people travelled to Britain from Western Europe. They were mainly farmers and village traders. Much of the countryside was covered with woodland. This woodland is known as the **Wildwood**. Some parts of the Wildwood still survive in Scotland. Skara Brae in the Orkney Islands has the remains of a village that dates from Stone Age times.

Remains of a Stone Age dwelling at Skara Brae

The farmers who came at that time cleared large areas of woodland and made fields for planting crops and keeping animals. They mined flint at places such as Grimes Graves in Norfolk. They made better quality stone tools from this. These Neolithic or New Stone Age people started to use bronze tools and weapons as time went on.

# Stonehenge

Neolithic men also built circles of **standing stones**. The best known of these is Stonehenge on Salisbury Plain in Wiltshire. Stonehenge is a group of huge, rough-cut stones set in circles. It was probably used as a tribal gathering place or a religious centre. Archaeologists have been able to work out what it looked like when it was first built. The largest standing stones rise four metres above the ground and weigh up to 25 tons each. Stonehenge was probably begun around 2700 B.C. and was built in different phases over the centuries up to 1500 B.C. Near the centre of the circle there was a flat block of sandstone almost five metres long. This could have been an altar. Historians who have studied the layout and design of Stonehenge believe that it was used to work out when important astronomical events would occur.

Stonehenge is a major tourist attraction today, with over one million visitors viewing it every year.

Stonehenge today

An artist's impression of how Stonehenge might have looked when it was built

# Exercise 3.1

Read the information on pages 19 to 22 about Prehistoric man and answer the following questions:

1. What were the earliest people who lived on earth called?

2. Where did the Southern Ape-man live?

3. Name three differences between the Southern Ape-man and Erect man.

4. What did Erect man use stone and wood for?

5. What is meant by the Ice Age?

6. Why is the Old Stone Age called the Old Stone Age?

7. What did Old Stone Age people eat?

8. Where did Stone Age people live?

9. Why do you think the use of fire was such an important discovery?

10. When did the last Ice Age end in Britain?

# Exercise 3.2

Read the information on pages 22 to 23 about the New Stone Age and complete the following sentences:

1. The New Stone Age started in around _____ B.C., in an area called the _____, on the banks of the Tigris and _____ rivers.

2. At this time, men became _____ rather than hunters.

3. Three main types of man developed in the different parts of the world: dark-skinned people lived in _____; white-skinned people lived in _____, _____ and _____; and yellow-skinned people lived in _____ and _____.

4. As a result of farming, the population began to grow. Extra food could be traded for other goods. This was called _____.

5. Clothes were made from _____ and _____. Houses were made from _____ and the roofs were thatched with _____.

· · · · · · · · · · · · · · · · · · · · · · · · · · · · · · · · · · · · · · · · · · · · · · · · ·

# Exercise 3.3

Look at pages 19 to 22 and then explain the following using your own sentences: .

1. prehistoric

2. homo erectus

3. hunter gatherers

4. neolithic

5. bartering

· · · · · · · · · · · · · · · · · · · · · · · · · · · · · · · · · · · · · · · · · ·

# To do

- Write a story of how you think the first Stone Age man discovered fire.

- Stone Age people made necklaces from mammoth teeth. Collect some wine bottle corks, colour them and make them into a necklace.

- Make your own cave painting. Use a straw to blow paint around your hand on a piece of paper, or use crayons or charcoal. Try to make it look like the pictures from Altamira on page 22.

# Chapter 4
# The Bronze Age

## Mesopotamia

We are now going to travel onwards in time, from the Stone Age to what we call the **Bronze Age**. You will soon find out why we call it the Bronze Age, but first you need to meet a people called the **Sumerians**. The Sumerians lived in the land between the Tigris and the Euphrates rivers which was known as **Mesopotamia**. They kept cattle, goats and sheep and built huts out of reeds. They used stone **hoes**, blades attached to long handles, to prepare

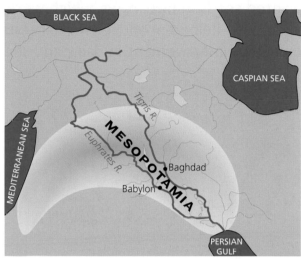

A map to show ancient Mesopotamia and the 'Fertile Crescent'

the soil for growing wheat and barley. The soil was very fertile because of the build-up of silt from the two rivers. These rivers flooded every year, making the nearby land into a swamp. Elsewhere, the soil was too dry for farming because there was very little rain. The Sumerians built huge banks along the Euphrates to stop it flooding. They dug canals and ditches, dams and reservoirs. These helped them guide the water to wherever it was needed. They were the first people to use this method, which is called **irrigation**.

The Sumerians traded their corn, dates, leather, wool and pottery with neighbouring countries. They brought timber, metals and semi-precious stones into Mesopotamia from abroad. The people became rich and villages grew into **towns** and **cities**. By 3500 B.C., cities such as Ur, Erech, Eridu, Lagash and Nippur existed. Each was kept rich and fertile by its own irrigation system.

Other inventions helped the progress of farming. The most important one was the **wheel**. The first wheel was made out of three pieces of wood joined together and bound with leather. **Oxen** were used to pull farm **carts** and other wheeled transport. The **ox-drawn plough** meant that fields could be prepared for planting using animal power. The **seed drill** planted seeds in neat rows, which were then covered up from behind. These inventions helped produce two harvests a year. More food for the animals meant an improvement in dairy and sheep farming.

The success of farming meant that some people could concentrate on crafts such as metalwork and pottery. They became experts at making sickles and pots which farmers exchanged for their corn and meat.

## Sumerian gods, priests and kings

The Sumerians believed that man had been created to supply the gods with food, drink and shelter. The Sumerians worshipped many gods and each city had its own patron god; for example, the chief god of Ur was called **Nannar**.

At the centre of each city was a **temple** which the Sumerians believed was where the patron god lived. This temple provided the god with shelter, but to provide him with food and drink the priests of the temple collected **taxes** from the people which paid for what the god needed.

The king of each city was thought to have been chosen by the god. He was responsible for governing the city well and making sure the irrigation system was kept working properly.

# The invention of writing

The Sumerians were the first people who learned to write. The first type of writing was called **cuneiform**, which means 'wedge-shaped'. This is because the priests used a piece of reed with a wedge-shaped end for a pen. The priests wanted to write because they needed to keep a record of all the taxes that they had collected. They scratched with the pen in tablets of clay and then baked these tablets so that they became hard. At first they drew pictures of objects, such as an ear of corn or a cow's head, with a number of dots or circles to show how many. Soon, however, these pictures became signs to stand for sounds rather than things. This was a big improvement. Instead of having to remember the picture for every single word they wanted to write, they could build up words by using a sign for each sound (or syllable).

However, they did not realise that these sounds could all be built up from a limited number of letters, as we do. Because of this, they did not have an alphabet and most Sumerians never learnt how to read and write.

# Sumerian learning

The Sumerians were very clever and were the first people to work out how to add, subtract and multiply. Their basic unit in mathematics was 60. That is why we have 60 minutes in an hour and 360 degrees in a circle. They also worked out a **calendar** based on the moon, with a year of twelve months.

Ancient cuneiform written on a clay tablet

They even wrote down some of their myths and legends on clay tablets and some of these have survived. One story tells of how Ziusudra built a great boat, or ark, and how this was tossed about on the waves for seven days and nights. Does this remind you of another story?

# The Bronze Age

Around 3500 B.C., someone in Sumeria discovered that a mixture of tin and copper gave a new material. This material was much harder than copper alone. We know it as **bronze**. Bronze objects such as ornaments, tools, vases and weapons have been found at **Ur**, the most famous Sumerian city. The **Bronze Age** had begun and lasted until iron tools became widespread.

In some areas, the Bronze Age lasted for a long time and in other areas it was very short. The first **helmets**, **swords** and **shields** were made from bronze. After some time, the supply of tin and copper found on the surface of the ground ran out. People then looked for metals under the ground and so mining began. Bronze weapons were better than stone weapons and people who had them became powerful. Bronze tools made life easier for farmers and wheels were made lighter and better by using spokes and a strip of bronze on the rim.

An artist's impression of the opencast mines on the Great Orme as they may have appeared around 2000 B.C.

# The smith

The person who made things from metal was called a **smith**. Smiths often kept their method of making objects a secret. They thus became important and powerful in Bronze Age times. They travelled from place to place searching for metals and swapping the items they made for other goods. A large amount of copper and a small amount of tin were heated in a container over the fire. When the metals began to melt they were mixed and poured into clay moulds of different shapes and sizes. When the metal cooled, the smith removed it from the mould and hammered out the edges to sharpen or smooth them.

# The Bronze Age in Britain

We have no written records from Bronze Age times in Britain. Our information comes from people's ornaments, tools and weapons. In about 1850 B.C., settlers from Europe first started to mine gold and copper in Britain. They are called the **Beaker Folk** because pots shaped like beakers have been found with their remains. The Beaker Folk discovered that tin and copper could be mixed to make bronze. By about 1700 B.C., Britain had entered the Bronze Age.

A Bronze Age woman wearing a lunula

Weapons, tools and jewellery from this time were very well made. The metals used were bronze, copper, tin and gold. They were mined mostly in Ireland, Wales and Cornwall. Jewellery included the **lunula**, a type of necklace shaped like a crescent moon and the **torc**, a rigid circular necklace that was open-ended at the front. Paper-thin gold discs were worn like brooches today.

A Bronze Age man wearing a torc

The powerful chieftains of **Wessex** (in southern England) took control of the **metal trade**. They sold metal objects to people in mainland Europe. The profits they made were used to buy rare goods. These included amber from the Baltic, blue beads from Egypt and gold objects from Greece. Many of these have since been found in round **barrows**, which were used to bury the dead.

# Where people lived

Bronze Age homes in Britain were round, oval or rectangular. They had stone walls and a thatched roof. They had one door and a hole in the centre of the roof. This was to let out the smoke from the fire. Cattle and pigs were kept inside the wall to protect them from robbers and wild animals.

A stone cottage with thatched roof at Culloden in the Scottish Highlands near Inverness

People also lived in **crannogs**. The name crannog comes from the Gaelic word 'crann', meaning 'tree'. A crannog was an artificial island, built on a lake or a bog. When a suitable site was found in a shallow part of a lake, a foundation of stones was laid. Earth, branches and wood were piled on top and an earthen floor was made.

It was circular in shape. Then a circle of timber posts was placed around the platform with lighter branches, called **wattles**, woven in and out through them. The houses were built inside this fence. The entrance from the shore to the crannog might have been a ladder or a drawbridge. Sometimes, a pathway was laid below the level of the water in a zigzag pattern. If you visit Loch Tay in Scotland, you will see a reconstruction of a crannog.

A crannog

# Food

Bronze Age people ate porridge made from wheat, barley and oats. They ate fish and pork more often than beef because cattle were considered very valuable. They hunted birds, rabbits, hares and deer. They also gathered wild fruit, berries and herbs. The **open fire**, the **spit** and the **cauldron** were all important for cooking. The people also cooked their meat in a rectangular pit lined with wooden planks or stone slabs. The pit was filled with water, which was heated by rolling hot stones into it from a fire close by. Meat was wrapped in straw and tied with straw rope. The wrapped meat was put into the boiling water and left to cook. Hot stones were added to keep the water on the boil. The hot stones often shattered on contact with the water. The broken stones were taken from the trough or pit and heaped to one side.

# Burial places

The great tombs of the New Stone Age and early Bronze Age were called **megaliths**, which means 'large stones'. The most common tomb during the Bronze Age was called a **Wedge Tomb** because it was lower and narrower towards the back. People stopped building tombs in the Bronze Age and buried their dead in **cists** instead. These were box-like shapes, made of stone slabs. Sometimes the bodies were cremated and the ashes were placed in the cist. Pottery and food vessels have been found in cists. Another type of grave was the **dolmen**. A dolmen was made up of three or more standing stones with a large slab of rock as a roof.

. . . . . . . . . . . . . . . . . . . . . . . . . . . . . . . . . . . . . . . . . . . . . .

# Exercise 4.1

Read the information on pages 27 to 29 and answer the following questions:

1. Where did the Sumerians live?

2. How did they guide water to where it was needed?

3. Name the invention of the Sumerians that most helped the progress of farming.

4. How did the ox-drawn plough and the seed drill help farmers?

5. What was the purpose of man, according to the Sumerians?

6. Who was the chief god of the city of Ur?

7. Where did the Sumerians believe their patron gods lived?

8. Why did the Sumerian priests need to write?

9. What was the basic unit in mathematics for the Sumerians?

10. Who or what was Ziusudra?

# Exercise 4.2

Read the information on pages 30 to 33 and complete the following sentences:

1. Around _____ B.C., the Sumerians discovered that a new material, _____, could be made by mixing two metals, _____ and _____.

2. The person who made things from metal was called a _____.

3. In about _____ B.C., settlers from Europe first started to mine _____ and _____ in Britain. They are called the _____ Folk.

4. By about _____ B.C., Britain had entered the Bronze Age.

5. The great tombs of the New Stone Age and early Bronze Age were called '_____', which means '_____'.

# Exercise 4.3

Explain the following using your own sentences:

1. irrigation

2. cuneiform

3. bronze

4. smith

5. crannog

# To do

- Cut out a lunula, a gold disc and a shield from cardboard and decorate them as people would have done in Bronze Age times.

- Tell a story about how you invented the wheel.

- Construct a Bronze Age dwelling using lollipop sticks, reeds, rushes, matchsticks and small stones.

# Chapter 5
# Ancient Egypt

When you think of Egypt, what do you think of? Perhaps you have seen the musical *Joseph* and think of the **pharaoh** and the **Nile**. The pharaoh was the name for the king of Egypt and the Nile is the big river that flows through **Egypt**. Egypt is in North Africa. Most of the land of Egypt is covered by a hot sandy desert called the Sahara. The River Nile is the second biggest river in the world. It flows through the Egyptian desert. Since ancient times, the people have lived along the banks of the river. Every summer it rained heavily

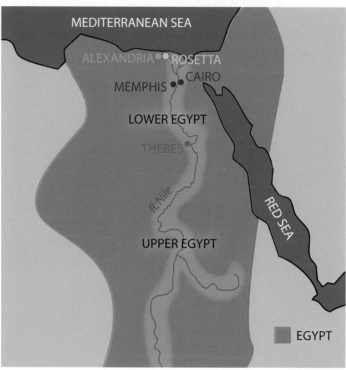

A map of Ancient Egypt

on nearby mountains. This caused the Nile to flood the land along its banks. The first settlers, in 5000 B.C., found this land to be like a swamp. A jungle of reeds hid dangerous animals like hippos and crocodiles and it was difficult to farm. With very little soil and a shortage of rainfall, a large part of Egypt was unsuitable for growing crops, so they used an irrigation system like the one used by the Sumerians. **Canals** drained floodwater from the banks and returned it during the dry months.

The floods left behind a covering of rich soil. This soil made the land very fertile, which was very good for growing crops and provided the Egyptians with large amounts of food. The number of people living along the banks increased because they had plenty of food. The reeds that grew in the shallow waters were used to make boats. Reed boats were used for travelling and larger wooden boats were used to move heavier loads. Mud from the riverbank was used to make clay bricks. The bricks were dried by the heat of the sun and were used to build houses.

The Nile valley was narrow and the villages on its banks were close together. Sometimes, arguments would break out between the villages. When this happened, the leader of one village might take control over the villages nearby. Later, these groups of villages joined together to form two kingdoms: Upper Egypt in the north and Lower Egypt in the south. The king of Upper Egypt wore a white crown. The king of Lower Egypt wore a red crown.

The White Crown of Upper Egypt

The Red Crown of Lower Egypt

# The pharaoh

In 3100 B.C. a king of Lower Egypt defeated the northern kingdom. He became the first pharaoh of Egypt. His name was **Menes**, or **King Narmer**. Narmer sometimes wore a white crown, sometimes a red. The pharaohs that came after Narmer wore a double crown that combined the white and red crowns from the north and south.

Ancient Egyptians believed that the pharaoh was a god who had come down to earth from the sky. Any order he made automatically became law. The pharaoh's government protected the land and its people from outside attacks. It also kept peace amongst the people. Anyone who broke the law was tried in a local **court**. The pharaoh's ministers acted as **judges**.

The pharaoh's government also looked after the irrigation system. When Egypt became one kingdom, the canals were brought together into one

big system. This was controlled from the capital, **Memphis**. By checking the level of the floods, the pharaoh's men could tell if a famine was coming. They prepared for famines by storing extra corn during good seasons. In the Bible, Joseph advised the pharaoh to do this and saved the Egyptians from famine as a result.

After the pharaoh in importance came the priests, the nobles, the merchants, the crafts-people, the farmers, the labourers and, finally, the slaves.

# Gods

The Egyptians worshipped many gods. Most of these were local gods but two gods were worshipped throughout all Egypt. One of these was the Sun god (**Horus** or **Ra**). The other was **Osiris**, god of the Nile and the afterworld. The pharaoh was believed to be the living Horus, or the son of Ra. When he died, it was thought he became one with Osiris. Later, the nobles and even the common people believed they too would become one with Osiris after their death. Osiris would judge them by their behaviour on earth and only the good would be granted life after death.

Osiris      Horus

# The pyramids

The pharaoh was very important in Egypt and thought to be a god, so the Egyptian people did not want him to die. They believed that the pharaoh's spirit could only survive if his body was preserved. Therefore, they had to keep his body safe and ensure that he had everything he might need in the afterlife. In preparation for this, the pharaohs built huge **tombs** which they filled with food, clothes, drink, jewellery, weapons, furniture and many other items. They had their favourite possessions and useful objects buried with them too.

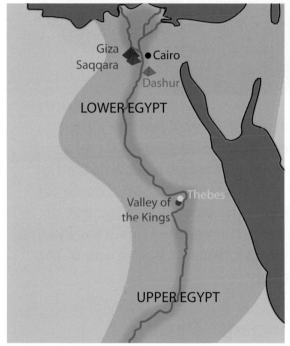

The Valley of the Kings

Pyramids at Giza

A map showing the location of the Valley of the Kings and the pyramids

Some pharaohs were buried in underground tombs in an area known as the **Valley of the Kings**. Others were buried in great stone tombs, called **pyramids**. The pyramids were built as homes for the dead pharaohs, allowing them to live forever. Thirty of these pyramids are still standing today and there are traces of thirty more.

The pyramids were built to last forever. The Egyptian people were charged high taxes to pay for them and, when we look at them now, we can see why. A typical pyramid consisted of a group of four buildings. There was a valley building, with a landing-stage on the river Nile. From this there was a covered walkway leading to a temple, dedicated to the dead pharaoh. This led on to the pyramid itself, which was surrounded by a high wall. Close to the main pyramid, inside the high wall, were smaller pyramids for the pharaoh's wives and daughters. Finally, outside the wall, tombs were built for the pharaoh's main ministers so that they could continue to serve their master. These were called **mastabas**.

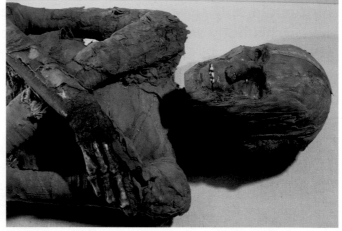
Mummified remains

The bodies of pharaohs were treated with special oils and wrapped in linen bandages. They are called **mummies** and some have survived until now.

The first pyramid was called the **Step Pyramid**. It was built by a man called Imhotep for his pharaoh, King Zoser, about 2600 years B.C. Although the Step Pyramid was an incredible achievement, it was small compared to the **Great Pyramid**, which was built for the pharaoh Cheops. The Great Pyramid is 146 m high and 229 m wide along each side. It is made out of 2 300 000 stone blocks, which weigh about 2½ tons each. The Great Pyramid is thought to have taken 100 000 men 20 years to make. It was one of the **Seven Wonders of the Ancient World**.

## The Seven Wonders of the Ancient World

The Ancient World was full of wonderful things, but seven of these were considered especially wonderful. You will learn about some of these in this course:

- The Great Pyramid of Giza
- The Hanging Gardens of Babylon
- The Statue of Zeus
- The Temple of Artemis
- The Mausoleum of Halicarnassus
- The Colossus of Rhodes
- The Lighthouse of Alexandria

# Tutankhamun

I'm sure you have heard of Tutankhamun. Tutankhamun was pharaoh of Egypt from about 1336 B.C. until his death in around 1327 B.C. He was nine years old when he was made Pharaoh and only a teenager of eighteen or nineteen when he died. His body was buried in a tomb in the Valley of the Kings at Thebes, which is known as Luxor today. His time as pharaoh was unimportant and it wasn't until his tomb was discovered that he became famous.

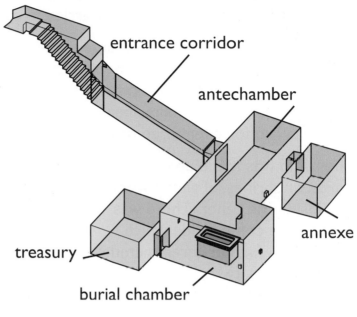

A 3D plan of the layout of Tutankhamun's tomb

Over the years, most of the tombs of the pharaohs were broken into by thieves, who stole the treasures within. Tutankhamun's tomb is the only tomb of an ancient Egyptian pharaoh to have been discovered almost completely undamaged. It was discovered by the British archaeologist **Howard Carter** in 1922. Howard Carter spent many years learning Egyptian history and searching for clues about the pharaohs. After almost ten years searching, he finally found the tomb of Tutankhamun. When Carter broke through the door of the tomb, he found himself in a passage about ten metres long. Rocks, sand and earth had fallen into this passage, almost blocking it. At the end of this passage was another sealed door. As Howard Carter broke through this door, he felt excited at what he might find, but anxious in case thieves had got there before him.

Suddenly, there it was. It was the most dazzling sight. The room was filled with the richest royal collection ever found. There were beautiful chariots, furniture and statues. There were vessels made of gold and silver, as well as beautiful pottery. There were models of animals and statues of Tutankhamun's guards and servants. He had been buried with everyday things, such as linen undergarments, a bronze razor, a board game and cases of food and wine. Models of ships, toys and storage jars containing precious oils were also found. The walls of the room were painted with the most beautiful of Egyptian pictures. Some showed Tutankhamun doing things such as eating, relaxing, hunting and fighting as a warrior in battle.

But where was the body? Two large statues stood against the end wall of the room, guarding another door. Behind this door was the actual burial place of Tutankhamun. On 26th November 1922, after years of searching in the Valley of the Kings, Howard Carter finally entered the room where the pharaoh's body had lain for over three thousand years.

The tomb was made up of four boxes, or shrines, of gilded wood, one inside the other. There was a red stone coffin inside which contained a further three mummy-shaped coffins, two gilded and one of solid gold. At the centre was the mummy of King Tutankhamun himself, with a stunning mask of gold covering his head and shoulders.

Inside Tutankhamun's burial chamber

The glitter of gold was everywhere. Precious collars, inlaid necklaces, bracelets, rings, amulets, an apron, sandals and many things of pure gold were found on the body. All the items were listed and photographed before being sent to museums. Most of the items are now displayed in the Egyptian museum in Cairo. The body itself was returned to the tomb where it had lain for over three thousand years.

# Using evidence

It may seem rather odd to us that the Ancient Egyptians thought that the pharaohs would need their bodies after their death. It may seem rather odd that they buried the dead with their possessions and decorated their tombs so beautifully. But, for historians, it gives us the most amazing snapshot of life in Ancient Egypt thousands of years ago. By examining the artefacts and the paintings that have survived in these ancient tombs, such as that of Tutankhamun, we are able to learn a great deal.

# Life for the nobles

From what has been found in the tombs of Ancient Egypt, we can build up a good picture of what life must have been like for the nobles and other rich people.

For example, we know that a rich man's house was large, often surrounded by a high wall. In the centre of the house was a large room, where the nobleman would entertain his guests. Leading off this room were private rooms and bedrooms for the family, each with their own bathrooms and lavatories.

Wall painting of a rich egyptian hunting, taken from the tomb chapel of Nebamun in Thebes New Kingdom c 1350 B.C.

The furniture was very similar to what we use today: beds, chairs, stools and tables all looked similar to our own furniture.

From the paintings, we can see that a nobleman would enjoy himself hunting for duck in the marshes of the river, or listening to music played on a harp, flute or lute. He might be rowed up and down the river, swim in the garden pool or play ball games with his children.

We also know that wealthy people wore stylish clothes and enjoyed dressing up. Men and women wore jewellery and used perfume. Women wore lots of make up as well as wigs. Dress was a way for wealthy people to show how important and powerful they were.

# Life for the peasants

Of course, the luxurious life enjoyed by the pharaohs and nobles was restricted to a very small portion of society. At the other end of the scale were the **peasants** who worked on the land, ploughing, sowing, watering the fields and gathering

Wall painting of a poor Egyptian from the tomb of Semedje

in the harvest. These peasants were often unpaid slaves and could be bought and sold by their rich masters. They lived in the houses of their masters or in their own small homes, made of sun-baked bricks.

Because of the hot climate, people wore light clothes. The men often simply tied a piece of cloth around their waists and the women wore linen dresses. Children might not wear any clothes at all.

# Everyday life

The river Nile provided the people with everything they needed. Wheat was grown along the riverbanks. This wheat was used to make bread, which was the main food for all Egyptians. They also ate fruit and vegetables, such as grapes, melons, beans and onions. They made wine from grapes and they also drank beer. They fished in the deep waters of the Nile and used nets and spears to catch the fish. Many ordinary people could not afford meat very often, but wealthy people could afford any food they liked. They ate lamb, goat and fowl. They had many different types of bread, fruit and nuts. For poorer people, life in Ancient Egypt was not so easy. Most people died by the age of thirty.

# School and playtime

Most children did not go to school but they learned many skills from their parents and neighbours. For example, they learned about fishing and farming in this way. They saw clay bricks, boats and baskets being made. Children went fishing, swimming and hunting. They kept pets, such as monkeys, cats and dogs. They played with wooden animals, spinning tops and dolls. They also enjoyed music and dancing.

The sons of the rich and powerful people went to school. There they learned to read and write. Children used pens made from reeds. Ink was made from soot or red earth and writing was done on **papyrus**. This was a type of paper made out of papyrus reeds, split into thin strips and stuck together. At first, their writing did not use letters and words. Instead of letters, they used picture signs called **hieroglyphs**. Each picture sign stood for an object or an idea. A sentence came about when a number of these picture signs were put in a row.

Later, they made these signs stand not for whole words, but for sounds, as the Sumerians had. Finally, they invented twenty-four signs to represent the simple sounds that made up all the syllables. These signs were like our letters, except that they did not have any vowels. And, to make things more complicated, they continued to use all the old signs as well, so it must have been very difficult indeed to read what had been written. Here are the twenty-four Egyptian sound-signs:

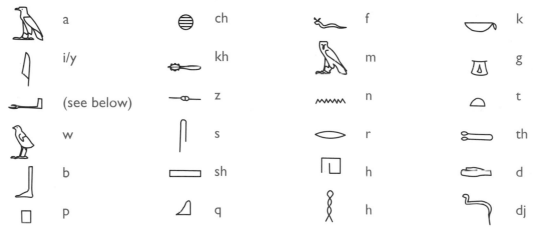

| | | | |
|---|---|---|---|
| a | ch | f | k |
| i/y | kh | m | g |
| (see below) | z | n | t |
| w | s | r | th |
| b | sh | h | d |
| p | q | h | dj |

These are the 24 signs that represent the different sounds when speaking. The third sign down on the left is the guttural sound you can produce, as if clearing your throat.

# The Rosetta Stone

Of course, it is very hard to read these ancient hieroglyphs and for thousands of years people couldn't understand them at all. But then, in 1799, a group of French soldiers found a stone at **Rosetta** in Egypt. It had three different types of writing on it: Greek, Egyptian and Demotic. Demotic writing was an Ancient Egyptian script developed in Lower Egypt. It had been carved in 196 B.C. by priests to honour their pharaoh. A man named Jean-Francois Champollion discovered what the writing said. Because he could read Greek and some of the Demotic writing, he managed to work out what the hieroglyphs stood for.

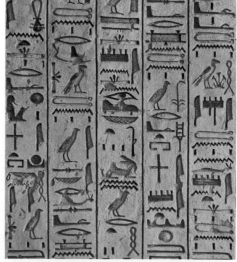

A sample of ancient hieroglyphs at the British Museum

# Exercise 5.1

Read the information on pages 36 to 42 and answer these questions:

1. Name the desert that covers most of Egypt.

2. When did the first settlers come to Egypt?

3. How did the Ancient Egyptians make the land around the Nile suitable for farming?

4. How were the Upper and Lower kingdoms of Egypt formed?

5. When was Egypt united under a single pharaoh, and what was his name?

6. What did the pharaoh's government do?

7. Name the capital of Ancient Egypt.

8. Name the two main gods worshipped in Ancient Egypt.

9. Why did the Ancient Egyptians build pyramids?

10. Who built the first pyramid, when and for whom?

11. Draw a diagram of a typical pyramid complex.

12. Name the Seven Wonders of the Ancient World.

13. When was Tutankhamun pharaoh?

14. When was Tutankhamun's tomb discovered, and by whom?

15. Why do you think the discovery of Tutankhamun's tomb has been useful to historians?

# Exercise 5.2

Read the information on pages 41 to 45 and fill in the following sentences:

1. Tutankhamun's tomb was discovered in the Valley of the Kings at _____ which was previously called _____.

2. A nobleman would enjoy hunting for _____ or listening to music played on a _____, _____ or _____.

3. Peasant women wore plain dresses made of _____.

4. Children used pens made from _____. Ink was made from _____ or red earth and writing was done on _____.

5. The Ancient Egyptians invented _____ signs to represent the simple sounds that made up all the _____.

6. In 1799 French soldiers found a stone at _____. A man called _____ discovered what the writing on the stone said.

# Exercise 5.3

Explain the following using your own sentences:

1. pharaoh

2. Osiris

3. pyramid

4. mummy

5. hieroglyphs

# To do

- Write a message using hieroglyphs.

- Imagine you are a child in Ancient Egypt. Write about a day in your life.

- Draw a picture of the Nile and show people doing their everyday jobs.

- Design a mask for a pharaoh like Tutankhamun.

- Find out as much as you can about the Seven Wonders of the Ancient World. Design a poster to display what you have found out.

# Chapter 6
# The spread of civilisation

## India

We have read about the beginning of civilisation in Egypt and the Near East. Another ancient civilisation grew up further east, in India. The soil there was very fertile. Some of the ideas about farming may have spread east from Mesopotamia to the **Indus Valley**. These ideas meant that by 2500 B.C. there was another group of people who were able to farm and live off their own land. We call them the **Indus Valley Civilisation**. Their farming was so successful that large numbers of people were able to live together, with enough food to feed them all, and they were able to build towns and cities.

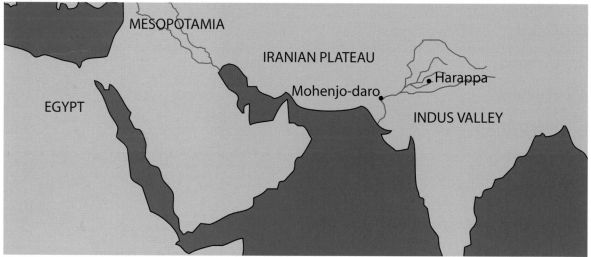

A map to show the Iranian Plateau and the Indus Valley

## Mohenjo-daro and Harappa

Evidence of about forty towns and cities inhabited by the Indus Valley people has since been discovered. The two about which we know the most are called **Mohenjo-daro** and **Harappa**. The ruins of these two cities are in modern day Pakistan. They may have been twin capital cities, Harappa in the north and Mohenjo-daro in the south. They were extremely well organised and carefully planned. Each was built beside a river. Straight streets divided the cities horizontally and vertically into squares. Mohenjo-daro was made up of twelve squares, with the **citadel** in the centre, surrounded by a wall.

Inside the wall there was a kind of monastery. We think that groups of powerful priests ruled over the cities, and that the citadel was their base. It also contained an enormous bath, used for **ritual bathing**.

The Indus Valley people were very keen on hygiene. They took baths by pouring water from large jars. Their **drainage** system was extremely effective. Every house had its own drain, which ran into a main **sewer** under the street. Rubbish was put into a chute, which passed through a wall into a large brick bin outside.

A reconstruction of Harappa

The chute from a two-storey house in Harappa

A covered drain emptying down a slope on a major street in Harappa

The wealthy people lived in large houses. Each house was built round a courtyard and contained rooms of different sizes. Some houses had one floor and some had two. The poorer workmen had to put up with small cottages with only two rooms. These were built close together in regular rows.

# Farming, trade and travel in Ancient India

Corn was regularly collected from the countryside as a form of tax. It was stored in granaries and ground in flour mills. Farmers also grew wheat, barley, peas and cotton. They kept buffaloes and bulls as well as domestic animals. They too developed crafts such as metalwork, pottery and brick-making.

They traded cotton, pepper and spices with nearby lands like Sumer.

Indians used camels and packhorses to get around and goats to take goods over the mountains. Heavy items were carried on carts. These had two wheels and were drawn by oxen. They were exactly the same as the ones still used in India today. Boats with a sail and a long oar were used for transport on water.

Some examples of transport in Ancient India

# Indian religion

The Indian people at this time were very religious. Many of their beliefs and customs have survived in **Hinduism** which is still the main religion in India. The name 'Hindu' comes from the Persian word for 'Indus'. A statue has been found from this time at Mohenjo-daro which looks just like the Hindu god **Shiva**. This discovery suggests that he was already being worshipped by then. Some people believe Shiva formed part of a trinity with two other gods, **Vishnu** and **Brahma**. Others think that he produced Vishnu, who in turn produced Brahma. Shiva is the god responsible for the destruction of evil in the world.

The Hindu god Shiva

Hinduism is the world's third largest religion. Hindus believe in **reincarnation** – that they will be reborn in a new form after they die. They also believe in **karma**: good deeds will bring good fortune, and evil actions will bring bad fortune. Most of all, Hindus are encouraged to be faithful to their own personal duties and values.

One of the religious customs that has been handed down from this first civilisation is ritual bathing. It is still practised in India today.

# China

Another very ancient civilisation was that of China. Chinese civilisation first began in the north of the country, along the valley of the **Yellow River**. The soil on its banks was very fertile from the silt left by flooding. This civilisation may be as old as those of the Near East, but we don't know anything about it until 1750 B.C. This was when the **Shang dynasty** kings started ruling China. A dynasty is a series of rulers who come from the same family. The Shang dynasty began when T'ang, a very wise man, overthrew the extravagant emperor Chieh, who was the last of the Hsia dynasty.

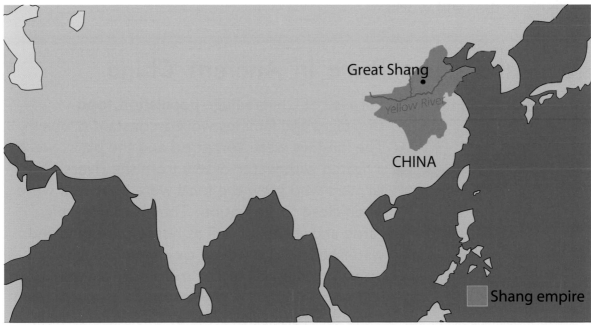

A map showing the location of the Shang dynasty at its greatest extent

One of the old capitals of the Shang dynasty was called **Great Shang**. Like Mohenjo-daro and Harappa it was well planned. It had a royal palace and many houses made out of wood, with pillars and gabled roofs.

Carpentry, stone-carving, pottery and bronze-working were all practised in China at this time. These crafts, as well as farming techniques, probably spread to China from the Near East.

The Shang worshipped a god called **Shang-Ti**, which means 'Most High Lord'. He ruled over the lesser gods of the sun, moon, wind and rain amongst others. The people believed their ancestors lived in heaven after death. They had to carry out certain duties to them or risk bringing trouble on the whole family. They performed **sacrifices** to the gods and to their

An archaeologist uncovers horse bones in the tomb of a Shang king

ancestors. After a king died, these could be human sacrifices. Archaeologists have found some of the tombs of the Shang kings. They were buried in enormous pits. Around the royal coffin, the bodies of many humans and horses were laid. They were killed so that they could keep the king company in the next world.

# Food and agriculture in Ancient China

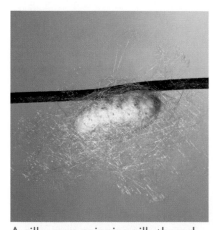

A silkworm spinning silk thread

Because of China's huge population, food shortages and famines were a constant problem. The hillsides were **terraced** and the plains were irrigated with water drawn from the rivers. The farmers who grew the food were poor and were often close to starvation. They kept dogs, pigs, cattle and sheep as well as horses, chickens and water-buffalo. They used ox-drawn ploughs and transported crops to the market by ox, donkey, mules and camels. They probably wove **silk** from the thread of silkworms by this stage as well.

Wheat, maize, rice and beans were the most popular crops. Poor people ate two meals a day. In the north, they ate cakes, some meat and eggs. In the south the main food was rice. Food was served in pottery bowls and eaten with chopsticks. Tea was the normal drink. The rich could afford a greater variety of foods, such as melons, pears and grapes. Important occasions were celebrated with feasts. Even though there was a great variety of food, the Chinese ate only a little for each course.

# Chinese discoveries and inventions

Ancient China was a place of great creativity. They invented **paper**, **gunpowder**, the first magnetic **compass**, the ship's **rudder** and **suspension bridges**. They designed **maps** using a grid system and they worked out that a year was 365¼ days. They used **paper money** and invented **printing**.

# Chinese characters

Information about the Shang dynasty comes from characters that have been found inscribed on bronze artefacts and oracle bones - turtle shells, cattle horns and other bones. People wrote questions on these, hoping to find out what would happen in the future. They provide the first examples of Chinese writing.

Later people used brushes to paint characters on silk. This gave the writer more freedom and the characters became more detailed and artistic. Originally the writing was **pictographic** – it was made up of symbols that looked like the things they stood for. Eventually it became more complex, but, even today, the Chinese do not really have an alphabet.

Ancient Chinese for 'fish'

Modern Chinese for 'fish'

Ancient Chinese for 'rain'

Modern Chinese for 'rain'

# Crete

As we have seen, the first civilisations were those of Sumer, Egypt, India and China. The people of western Europe were still living very basic lives for thousands of years after civilisation had spread to these parts. The Greek island of Crete was the part of Europe closest to the Near East, so civilisation reached there first. We know that the island was first colonised in about 5000 B.C. by people from Western Asia. Roughly 2000 years later Egyptians arrived, bringing their knowledge and ideas to the Cretans. Even though they learnt a lot from other countries, the Cretans developed a unique civilisation unlike any other.

# The story of the Minotaur

One of the most famous stories from this Greek civilisation on Crete is that of Theseus and the Minotaur. Half bull, half man, the Minotaur was a fearsome monster with a taste for human flesh. It lived in the **labyrinth**, a great maze of winding passages at Knossos in Crete. Each year seven youths and seven maidens were sent from Athens as food for the beast.

Theseus was the greatest of the Athenian heroes. He said he would go to Crete and fight the monster. His father Aegeus was unsure. He remembered how others had been killed by the beast. Theseus insisted. He rigged his ship with black sails. This was the custom when Greeks were sailing to meet their doom. Theseus promised to hoist white sails on his return to show that he had succeeded.

Theseus's ship arrived at the harbour of Knossos, near the palace of King Minos of Crete. He met the king's daughter, Ariadne, and fell in love with her. Theseus told Ariadne that he was going to kill the Minotaur. She decided she would help him. She knew that even a hero would get lost in the winding passages of the labyrinth, so she gave him a ball of thread. "Unwind it as you go in. You will be able to find your way out again by following the thread," she explained. So Theseus entered the dark, winding labyrinth, undoing the thread as he went.

Soon he heard the bellowing beast. As he walked on, the roars got louder and louder until Theseus was at the centre of the maze and face to face with the monster. He paused, waiting for the best moment to attack. As the creature turned his back, Theseus sprang, plunging his sword into the beast's flesh. The Minotaur gave out one last bellow and breathed its last. Theseus found his way out of the maze using Ariadne's thread. He sailed quickly back to Greece to tell his father that he had succeeded. He was so excited, however, that he forgot to hoist his white sails. When Aegeus saw his son's ship rigged with the black sails he feared the worst. The old man, despairing, flung himself from the cliff into the seas and drowned in the waves below. Theseus had won his victory but lost his father.

# Discoveries of Arthur Evans

The story of Theseus and the Minotaur is one of many Greek **myths**. A myth is a story and surely we should not be expected to believe such a fantastical story. Or should we? An archaeologist named **Sir Arthur Evans** discovered that there might be some truth in the story.

Sir Arthur Evans was born in 1851. His father was a well known collector of ancient objects and, in 1894, Arthur travelled to Crete where he spent several years digging at **Knossos**. What he found was the ruins of a palace, so complicated that it might have seemed like a maze or labyrinth to those who visited it. It occupied an area of more than 5½ acres and contained over a thousand rooms and apartments, on five different levels. Although the palace is in ruins, it is still possible to see the colourful frescoes painted on the walls. These show plants, animals and people, and tell us a great deal about the people who lived in the palace.

Sir Arthur Evans rebuilt large sections of the palace and his work gives us a good idea of how it must have looked. It seems that, over the years, the palace suffered on several occasions from earthquake damage and also from fire.

For historians, the discovery of the palace at Knossos is very exciting because it allows us to piece together bits of the jigsaw puzzle that is the past.

One discovery has proved particularly interesting. You remember that, in the story of Theseus, the seven boys and seven girls were fed to a bull-like creature called the Minotaur. Well, one painting in the palace at Knossos

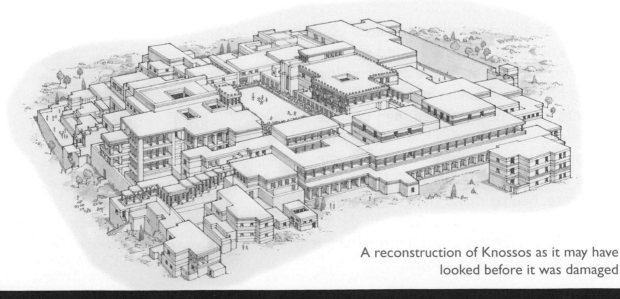

A reconstruction of Knossos as it may have looked before it was damaged

suggests that this may not have been just a story. It shows a huge bull with three figures. Two of them seem to be controlling the bull, and a third is jumping over the bull's back.

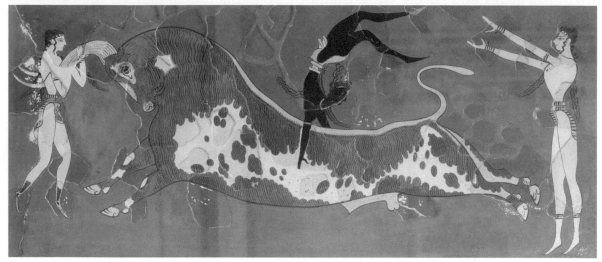

The bull leaping fresco from the palace at Knossos

This 'sport' of bull leaping would have been very exciting to watch, but imagine how dangerous it would have been! No doubt, there would have been a constant need for new acrobats willing to take part. Maybe that is why King Minos was so keen to receive the seven boys and seven girls from Athens every year. And maybe the Minotaur was not an imaginary monster, but a wild bull, used for this spectacular sport.

# Trade

Crete was a very heavily populated country. It was known as 'hundred-citied Crete'. The farmland was not as fertile as the valleys of the Near East, China and India and the farmers could not grow enough corn to feed everyone and raise the money needed to build cities. Instead, the Minoans, the name for the people who lived at this time on Crete, had to make things and sell them to other countries. Therefore, all the great cities were near the coast from where it was easier to export goods.

Various vessels and domestic utensils made by the famous Cretan potters

The Cretans sold cloth woven from sheep's wool and goods crafted from ivory, gold, silver and bronze. They were most famous for their pottery, however. The potters made all types and sizes of vessels. They made small cups as well as giant vases up to six feet high, often beautifully decorated. They were painted with birds and plants, shells and starfish.

Cretan goods were exported to many different countries around the Mediterranean. We know that the Egyptians bought bronze goods, precious metal bowls and pottery vases. In exchange, the Cretans took papyrus, linen and spices. The goods traded were carried by Cretan ships. Minoan sailors were probably the first to sail regularly across the Mediterranean and Crete, and as well as being a very successful trading country, was also the first big sea-power in history.

# Minoan writing

In 1936, Sir Arthur Evans gave a lecture in London to tell people all about the discoveries he had made in Crete. At this lecture he talked about the many clay tablets that he had found with markings on them. It was clear that these markings were some sort of writing, but no one was able to work out what the markings meant.

Minoan markings on the Phaitos disk

Evans worked out that there were two distinct types of writing, and he called these **Linear A** and **Linear B**. For many years they remained a complete mystery until a man called **Michael Ventris** managed to decipher the writing known as Linear B. He discovered that the markings recorded lists of stores, taxes and soldiers and that the language they were written in was a very early form of Greek. No one has ever managed to decipher Linear A. Perhaps one day you will do so!

A sample of Linear A script

# Exercise 6.1

Read the information on pages 48 to 53 and answer the following questions:

1. Where are the ruins of Mohenjo-daro and Harappa?

2. Describe Mohenjo-daro in your own words.

3. What evidence do we have that the Indus Valley people were keen on hygiene?

4. Why was corn very important in the Indus Valley?

5. What is the main religion of India and what connection does it have with Mohenjo-daro?

6. What important beliefs do Hindus have?

7. Where did the Chinese civilisation first begin?

8. When did the Shang dynasty begin?

9. What were the important foods in ancient China?

10. What important discoveries and inventions did the Chinese leave behind?

. . . . . . . . . . . . . . . . . . . . . . . . . . . . . . . . . . . . . . . . . . .

# Exercise 6.2

Read the information on pages 53 to 56 and fill in the following sentences:

1. The island of Crete was first colonised in about _____ B.C.

2. The Minotaur lived at _____ in a great maze.

3. The greatest of the Athenian heroes was _____, who killed the Minotaur.

4. Sir Arthur Evans discovered the ruins of a huge _____ in Knossos.

5. Cretans could not produce enough corn for their large population because the land was less _____ than in the Near East, China or India.

# Exercise 6.3

Explain these words using your own sentences:

1. citadel

2. ritual

3. dynasty

4. sacrifice

5. terraced

. . . . . . . . . . . . . . . . . . . . . . . . . . . . . . . . . . . . . . . .

# To do

- Find out what you can about the Hindu religion and make a wall chart to display in your classroom.

- Draw a strip cartoon to tell the story of Theseus and the Minotaur.

- Invent your own alphabet. Design your own letters and then write a message using your alphabet. Give it to a friend and see if they can decipher it.

# Chapter 7
## The Iron Age

## War and invasion

The civilisations we have learnt about so far all grew up in areas where the land was fertile. In other parts of the world, however, lived people who were jealous of the fertile farmland of the new civilisations. Soon these civilisations came under threat of invasion by uncivilised peoples from all sides. The first to be overcome was Sumer.

The main threat to Sumer came from a people called the **Akkadians**. The Akkadians were part of the **nomadic** (wandering) tribes from the Syrian and Arabian deserts. These tribes were all of **Semitic** blood, ancestors of the Arabs and the Jews. They began by invading Mesopotamia. This area became known as **Akkad**. Then they moved down to Sumer itself, taking over one city-state after another. They were led by a man named **Sargon**.

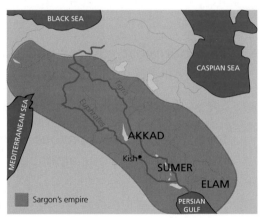

A map showing the extent of Sargon's empire

Sargon didn't stop there. He and his men marched down into Elam, beyond the river Tigris. Then he travelled north to the Euphrates, conquering as he went. Eventually, he had invaded all the land from the Mediterranean to the Persian Gulf. He was the first man in history to have an **empire**. An empire is a number of different countries, ruled over by the same person or group of people.

For 2000 years, changes like this continued to happen everywhere. Violent, primitive tribes moved into the old civilised lands. The original inhabitants were not killed but had to give in to being ruled by the newcomers. Their wealth and cities were taken over. Over time, the conquering people came to respect and admire the civilised ways of these old nations. They dropped some of their own backward ways and took on new customs. For example, Sargon's people started living in houses instead of in the tents of the desert. They learnt to write using cuneiform signs.

Hammurabi's pillar

In about 1750 B.C., a Semitic leader called **Hammurabi** became king of the Mesopotamian empire which, from this time, came to be known as **Babylonia**. Hammurabi was very organised and keen on justice and order. He collected together the old laws of the Semites and the Sumerians. He arranged them in order and added to them. There were almost 300 laws in total. He had them carved on a large stone pillar, in cuneiform writing. At the top of the pillar a picture of him was carved, standing in front of the Babylonian Sun god. This was to show that the laws were approved by the gods.

The introduction of formal laws was an important part of the progress of civilisation. Punishments included fines, money paid for committing a crime and more severe punishments were handed out for crimes against rich people.

# Indo-Europeans

Elsewhere, another group of people were posing a threat to civilisation. They were known as the **Indo-Europeans** and were even tougher and better fighters than the Semites. They came from southern Russia. They were nomads who were constantly moving to find fresh grass for their horses. They fought in **horse-drawn chariots**, with wooden frames and spoked wheels. Each was drawn by two horses, so they travelled very fast. They contained a driver and a warrior, who did the fighting.

An artist's impression of an Indo-European horse-drawn chariot

The Indo-Europeans began to invade south-western Asia from about 2000 B.C. The first group to arrive was the **Hittites**. The native people had no defence against the chariots of the Hittites. The Hittites fought their way through the land around the Black Sea and the Caspian. Eventually they had a large empire covering the area of Asia Minor.

## The invention of iron

We think that it was the Hittites who first discovered iron. Bronze was rare and expensive, but iron was cheap and there was lots of it. At the time, it was mainly used to make weapons. Armies became better equipped and fighting became more terrible. It had a positive purpose too, however. It was used to make cheap tools, which were of benefit to farmers and craftsmen.

This period is called the **Iron Age**. It began in about 1200 B.C. in the Near East and gradually spread to other parts of the world.

## The Mycenaeans

Other Indo-European peoples followed the Hittites. In 1500 B.C., the **Aryans** invaded India and attacked the Indus Valley civilisation, which had grown weak. At the same time, the **Achaean Greeks** were defeating the Minoan civilisation. They entered eastern Europe and eventually took over the whole Greek peninsula.

We know from Evans's findings at Knossos that the civilisation on Crete came to an abrupt, perhaps violent end. The palace was damaged by fire and it may be that the people of Crete faced attack from these invading Achaeans.

An artist's impression of the downfall of Knossos

Around this time, the Minoan civilisation was replaced by a civilisation which we call **Mycenaean**. Greece is a very mountainous country and during this period a number of small kingdoms grew up, cut off from one another by the mountains. The main kingdoms were those of **Mycenae**, **Thebes**, **Athens** and **Sparta** and the civilisation took its name from the first of these, Mycenae. We know that the warriors who lived in these kingdoms were fierce and warlike. But how do we know this?

# Homer and the mask of Agamemnon

To answer this question we need to introduce you to a blind poet called **Homer**. Homer lived around 700 B.C., long after the time of the Mycenaeans. But he is important because he told tales of the Mycenaeans which had been passed down from father to son until, many centuries later in Homer's time, they were written down. The two poems for which Homer is famous are called the **Iliad** and the **Odyssey** and are among the finest works of poetry ever composed.

# The Iliad

The *Iliad* tells the story of an episode during the **Trojan War**. King Agamemnon of Mycenae went to war with King Priam of Troy to rescue the beautiful Queen Helen. Helen, the wife of King Menelaus of Sparta, had run away to Troy with Paris, son of the Trojan king, and Agamemnon organised a Greek army to recover her. For ten years this army fought with the Trojans but, however hard they tried, they could not capture the city.

In the tenth year of the war, Agamemnon had a furious argument with the mighty warrior Achilles. Achilles refused to fight for the Greeks and the Trojan army rejoiced. Eventually, however, Achilles was persuaded to return to the fighting and, in a terrible duel, he killed the Trojan warrior Hector, tied him by the ankles to the back of his chariot and dragged him back to his camp.

It was then that the crafty Odysseus, a Greek warrior, had the plan of building a wooden horse. Inside the horse he hid a fighting force of Greek soldiers and the rest of the Greeks then pretended to sail away, back to Greece. The Trojans dragged the horse into the city and, in the night, the Greek soldiers poured out. Troy was burnt to the ground, and the Greeks sailed back home victorious with their ships full of slaves, including the beautiful Helen – Helen of Troy as she is now known.

## The Odyssey

In the *Odyssey* we hear how, after the war, Odysseus sailed back towards his home on the island of Ithaca. On his way home he faced many dangers: he was nearly eaten alive by Polyphemus, a one-eyed Cyclops who imprisoned him in a cave. He had to sail between the twin dangers of Scylla (a wild dog-like creature that lived on a rock face) and Charybdis (a fearsome whirlpool). He escaped from the witch, Circe, who turned his men into pigs, and from the enchantress, Calypso, who kept him on her island for seven years.

For ten long years Odysseus wandered over the seas, desperate to return home. When eventually he did return, it was to find that his loyal wife Penelope was being kept prisoner in her own house by a group of suitors who all wanted to marry her and take over her property. Odysseus, disguised as a beggar, managed to overcome these suitors and was reunited at last with his wife.

# Myth or history?

These stories were told down the ages by **bards**, travelling poets who told stories of heroes, accompanied by the **lyre**, a stringed musical instrument. Homer may have been such a man, a bard or **minstrel**, with a peculiar gift for telling memorable stories and setting them to beautiful poetry. In doing so, he revealed details of the times he was describing, details which have proved very useful to historians of this period. One such man was the German archaeologist **Heinrich Schliemann**. Schliemann was convinced that the stories Homer told were true, or largely based on truth, and he set out to prove it.

# Schliemann in Troy

Schliemann was born in 1822 and had a life-long ambition to discover the ancient city of Troy. Between 1870-1873 he carried out extensive digs at a place called **Hissarlik** in Turkey where he found the remains of an ancient city which had been burnt and destroyed. Here he found artefacts and treasures which immediately persuaded him that he had found the treasure of King Priam: cups, plates, necklaces, bracelets and over 8000 gold rings.

The gold mask of Agamemnon

We now know that the city Schliemann discovered was the remains of nine different cities, built one on top of the other over the ages, going back to around 3000 B.C. Whether we believe Homer's account of the fall of Troy or not, it seems likely that there was indeed a great city and that it was attacked – probably several times – and destroyed. Once again, the myths we read seem to be closely linked to historical truth.

# Schliemann in Mycenae

Excited by his discoveries in Troy, Schliemann then moved to Greece and from 1876 started extended excavations at the ancient site of Mycenae. He soon found what he was looking for: the graves of five warriors, surrounded with gold ornaments, weapons, cups and plates. One of the bodies lay concealed beneath a wonderful, golden mask which Schliemann took to be that of King Agamemnon himself. "I have looked upon the face of Agamemnon," he said, although we now know that these bodies were hundreds of years older than the hero of Homer's tale.

Schliemann's excavations at Mycenae, and those of other archaeologists who followed him, revealed evidence of an immensely rich and powerful city. The entrance to this city is known as the 'Lion Gate' because of the magnificent sculpture of two lions above it.

The 'Lion Gate' at Mycenae

Other indications that the city was the strongest and richest in all of Greece include the Mycenaeans' secret water supply within their defences, which came from an underground spring just outside. The city contained a number of huge, old-fashioned beehive-shaped tombs. One well known tomb (the Treasury of Atreus) measured nearly 15 metres in diameter.

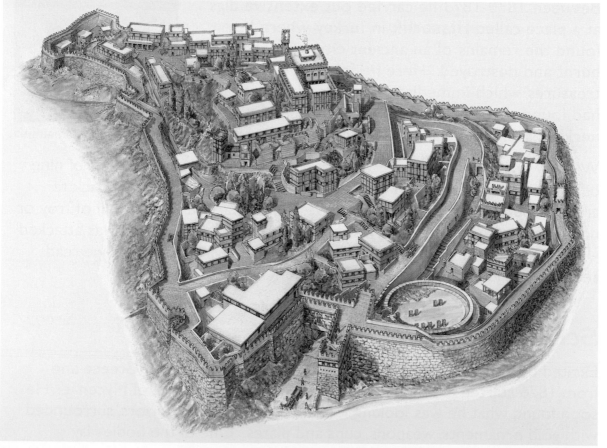

A reconstruction of Mycenae. Can you see the 'Lion Gate'?

Homer used the word 'golden' to describe Mycenae, which was a suitable description, as more gold has been found there than in all the other ancient Greek sites put together. Mycenae's arts and fashions, weapons and pottery were exported and copied all over the known world, to such an extent that this period of Greek history, the Mycenaean Age, takes its name from this one great city.

# Exercise 7.1

Read the information on pages 60 to 64 and answer these questions:

1.  What was the first civilisation to be overcome by foreign invaders?

2.  Who was the leader of the Akkadians?

3.  Name two ways in which the Akkadians were influenced by the Sumerians.

4.  Who introduced a set of laws in Babylonia in 1750 B.C.?

5.  How many horses drew the chariots of the Indo-Europeans?

6.  Who do we think first discovered iron?

7.  What was iron used for?

8.  Name the four kingdoms in Greece.

9.  Who was Homer?

10. What is the *Iliad*?

# Exercise 7.2

Read the information on pages 63 to 67 and complete the following sentences:

1.  In the tenth year of the Trojan War_____ had a furious argument with the mighty warrior _____.

2.  _____ came up with the plan of hiding the Greek army inside a wooden _____.

3. _____ was burned to the ground and the _____ sailed home victorious.

4. Schliemann carried out extensive digs at _____ in Turkey and discovered treasure including _____ gold rings.

5. The city Schliemann discovered was the remains of _____ different cities reaching back to around _____ B.C.

6. The entrance to the city of Mycenae is known as the '_____ _____', due to a sculpture of two _____.

7. Homer described Mycenae as _____ and this period of Greek history is known as the _____ Age.

## Exercise 7.3

Explain these words using your own sentences:

1. nomadic

2. Semitic

3. empire

4. laws

5. bard

## To do

• Find out more about the 'Lion Gate' of Mycenae and make a picture of it.

• On a map of the world, see if you can find which places were invaded and overcome during the Iron Age. Where did the invaders come from? Mark their routes on the map with ribbon or coloured string.

• Imagine you are the ruler of a new country. What laws would you make? How would you make sure people obeyed them?

# Chapter 8
# The Greek Dark Ages

## The Dorian invasions

For some reason, the Mycenaean civilisation went into decline between 1200 and 1100 B.C. The population of their once great cities dwindled quickly, until there was no urban culture left on the Greek mainland. Most of the cities were destroyed and all their great craftsmen left because there were no people to support them.

This period may be as a result of the migrations and invasions of a people called the **Dorians**. The Dorians were a tribe of ancient Greeks. They lived in the northwest of Greece. They swept down from the mountains and took over most of the **Peloponnese**, which is the large, southern peninsula of Greece. The Dorians went on to settle in **Argos**, **Corinth** and **Rhodes**. As they took over southwest Greece, they destroyed many cities.

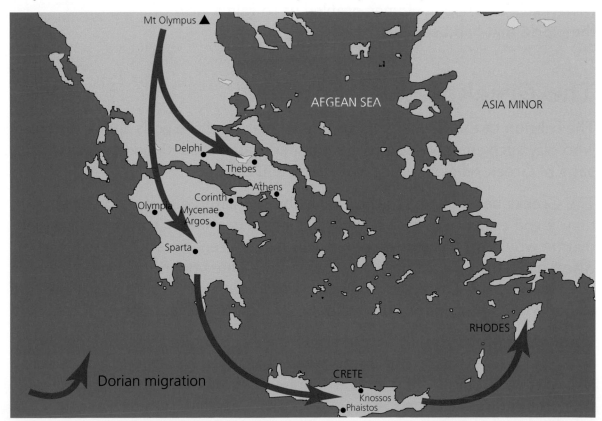

A map to show how the Dorians migrated from the mountains of the north to the island of Rhodes

In the same way as Troy was destroyed by the Mycenaeans, the Mycenaeans in turn may have been destroyed by the Dorians. In the period that followed, from 1200 to 700 B.C., people seem to have abandoned writing. With no writing, they left us no written history. All we have is five centuries of mystery. We call this period the **Greek Dark Ages**.

## The Dark Ages

After the Dorian invasion, many people from Mycenae fled from Greece. Some crossed the Aegean Sea and settled in Asia Minor, which became known as **Ionia**. During this time people lived in isolated villages. Written stories did not appear again for hundreds of years but, even though writing was forgotten, many tales of the past were kept alive through songs and poetry, passed down from generation to generation. Eventually, when the Greeks returned to the art of writing that had been lost, the remarkable blind poet, Homer, enabled us to gain a view of the world that had been lost.

Homer

## The Greek view of creation

The religion of the Greeks survived these years and the gods and goddesses, who play such an important part in Homer's poems, continued to form the basis of Greek religion during and after the Dark Ages.

The Greeks believed that the world had been created out of chaos. After a time, a god called **Cronos** became ruler of the heavens. Cronos was worried that he would be overthrown one day by his children. So every time his wife **Rhea** had a baby, he ate it! This went on for a time until Rhea tricked him. She hid one baby, **Zeus**, and wrapped a small boulder in a cloth which she gave to her wicked husband. Cronos swallowed the boulder and Zeus escaped.

Zeus was brought up on the island of Crete by a she-goat and, when he was older, he climbed up Mount Olympus and challenged his father. Cronos was forced to vomit up all the babies whom he had swallowed and, miraculously, they were quite unharmed. Cronos was then expelled from heaven and Zeus ruled in his place.

# Greek religion

As ruler of the heavens, Zeus gave jobs to all of his brothers and sisters. Each god represented some aspect of nature. Zeus himself was the god of the sky. His sister **Hera**, whom he married, was queen of the gods, and goddess of marriage. **Apollo** was the god of music and light. **Athene** was the goddess of wisdom and **Ares** the god of war. **Aphrodite** was the goddess of love and **Poseidon** was the god of the sea.

The Greeks believed that their gods could foretell the future. People visited shrines called **oracles** to talk to priests and priestesses. It was thought that the gods spoke to the people through the priests. This could have disastrous results, as the tale of Oedipus shows.

# The story of Oedipus

Once upon a time, there was a king of Thebes called Laius. One day, Laius visited an oracle and was told that he would be killed by his own son. Not wishing to be killed, Laius pinned his baby son's feet together and ordered that he be left on the mountainside to die.

However, the slave who was to have left the baby to die took pity on him and gave him to a shepherd. This shepherd, in turn, gave the baby to Polybus, the king of Corinth. Polybus named the child Oedipus and brought him up as if he were his own. His real father, Laius, believed that the boy was dead.

When Oedipus grew up, he went to visit the oracle at Delphi. This oracle told him that he would murder his father and marry his mother. Horrified at this, the young man left his home in Corinth and travelled to Thebes. On the way he met an old man. A fight took place and Oedipus killed the old man, although he did not know who he was.

Oedipus then travelled on to Thebes, where he fell in love with a lady called Jocasta. Jocasta had been married to the old man but, again, Oedipus did not know this.

Some time later, Oedipus became king of Thebes and everyone loved him. But a curse descended on the city and it slowly became clear what had happened: the old man that Oedipus had killed was none other than Laius, his own father. The lady he had married was none other than his own mother. The oracle's prophecy had come true.

## The Olympic Games

The Greeks lived in small, independent cities but were united by a common language, Greek, and by a common religion. Religious festivals were held every year in honour of the gods. At these festivals large crowds gathered. Feasts, colourful processions and performances of plays took place.

They also shared a love of athletics. We know that athletics was popular during the Dark Ages from the poems of Homer. For example, when Achilles's friend Patroclus was killed in the *Iliad*, games were held in his honour. Athletes competed in such events as wrestling, boxing, foot and chariot races, jumping and javelin throwing.

Athletics was seen as being part of religion. Several religious festivals brought together people from throughout the Greek world. The most famous of these festivals took place every four years at **Olympia** in honour of Zeus. The first games were held there in 776 B.C. and

the Olympic Games are still popular today. Athletes from throughout the Greek world would compete at these games, and wars would stop while the competitors took part. The victors received a crown of laurel leaves.

# The spread of Greek cities

During the Greek Dark Ages, perhaps because of the dangers brought by the invading Dorians, a large number of Greeks fled their homeland and settled elsewhere in the Mediterranean area. Perhaps they also left in search of more fertile land to farm. Between 750 and 600 B.C., a large number of Greeks settled along the coast of Asia Minor. These people, wherever they lived, always looked back with fondness to their motherland in Greece. Over the next few hundred years, the influence of Greece spread and we now look back on the age of Greece as the foundation of our own civilisation. In the next book in this course you will learn all about these people and the Romans who came after them.

· · · · · · · · · · · · · · · · · · · · · · · · · · · · · · · · · · · · · · · · · · ·

# Exercise 8.1

Read the information on pages 69 to 71 and answer the following questions:

1. When did the Mycenaean civilisation go into decline?

2. Why did the craftsmen leave?

3. Why is the period 1200 to 700 B.C. called the Dark Ages?

4. Where did some of the people who fled from Greece at this time go and live?

5. How were many tales of the past kept alive, even when writing was abandoned?

6. Which god emerged from chaos to become ruler of the heavens?

7. Where and how was Zeus brought up?

8. Whom did Zeus marry?

9. Of what was Apollo the god?

10. Why did people visit oracles?

# Exercise 8.2

Read the information on pages 71 to 73 and complete the sentences below:

1. Laius, the King of _____, was told by an oracle that he would be killed by his_____.

2. Oedipus visited the oracle at _____, then travelled to _____, where he fell in love with a lady called Jocasta.

3. The Greeks lived in small independent cities but were united by a common _____ and a common _____.

4. Achilles's friend _____ had games held in his honour. These included events such as _____.

5. Athletics was seen as part of _____. The most famous festival took place at _____ every four years.

· · · · · · · · · · · · · · · · · · · · · · · · · · · · · · · · · · · · · · · · · · · · · · · · · · ·

# Exercise 8.3

Explain these words using your own sentences:

1. isolated      4. processions

2. oracle      5. victors

3. festival

· · · · · · · · · · · · · · · · · · · · · · · · · · · · · · · · · · · · · · · · · · · · · · · · · · ·

# To do

- Write a story about life in the Greek Dark Ages. Try to imagine what life would have been like. You could pretend that you were the only person in your village who knew how to write and was able to record what was happening.

- Find pictures of the Greek gods and then make a poster of them all.

- Write a newspaper article about Oedipus.